I AM

By
Ushaa

Kaizer

And

Hde

team.

matthew,
Rudy,
Rhakam,Pierre-
Yves
Ulysse velky
,Maxima and
all hde.

Be

yourself

Most

people

use 90

percent

of their
time to
trying to
have
thing

rather

to «be»

we

«are»

human

the verb «be» Is forgotte n.

You are a being. What we call GOD IS

THE
ULTIMA
TE
PRESEN
CE THE

I AM and we are that I AM

If

you

want

use

your

potentia
l to the
fullest
you
must be

totally

present

in what

we call

the

instant. This moment in the present,

not the

future

not the

past

.

Just here and now. Take a

deep
breath.
And
prepare
your

self for
the
revelati
on

,

of
yourself
. 95
percent
of you

life and
day are
under
control
of your

subcons

cious

mind.

What

that

mean? You are
not free. But you
can be

now,und

erstand

that

everythi

ng that

you

think

that you

are you

become

This is the power of I AM. Your

**subcons
cious
mind
believe
what**

you say
about
yourself

.

When

you say
I
AM.........
somethi
ng You

start a

new

mechan

ism of

unconsc

ious
thought. You are
not

present.

You are not aware. You are anxious

or
stresse
d. Do
you
regret

the past
or do
you
worry
about

the
future?
But now
take a
deep

breath

we

enter in

a new

dimensi

onal world, we enter in the

present » in the «presen ce» in the «I

am»
LOVE
YOURS
ELF
Accept

you,
love
you,
now and
forever..

.. We will make new affirmat

ion for

your

mind

Take

seriousl

y this
exercis
e and
you will
leave

old

world

and

habits

and you

will live

in a

world of

grace

and

light. I
AM
LOVE I
AM love
and I

radiate
Love.
Love is
abunda
nt and I

AM THE

ABUND

ANCE I

AM

RICH

and

wealth

is

already

inside

me and

i don't

need to

found

external

evidenc
e of my
wealth
All the
treasure

,are in
myself.
Open
your
eyes

and be
in the
moment
,the sun
shine,

take a

deep

breath,

you are

safe in

this

eternal

moment

. Being

the "I

AM" Is being in the eternal present.

GOD BEING IS «I AM THAT, I AM»

You create your destiny with the

word I
am look
those
who
said «I

am

poor»

They

become

poor.

If
you
change
the
word

after

the I am

you

attract

another

Reality. You are the presence of God

I am that, I am MEAN that

God are the I am all who exist Is God.

You are this presence, and can

create whatev er you want. WHO

ARE YOU? You are the presenc

e of the
univers
e You
are the
God you

always
pray
since
you are
a young

child. You are the presenc e but

the only
place
that you
can be
the God

« lam

» that

you are

Is in the

present. The more you give is the

more

you

receive

you are

the

mirror
of the
univers
e. You
are the

reflectio
n of you
inside.
GIVE
LOVE

GIVE JOY GIVE and you will

always
in a
reality
of

Love,Jo

y, AND
ABUND
ANCE.
Why
don't

you see
yourself
as the
presenc
e of

God? Becaus
e they teach
you that

God is in the sky and control everythi

ng. The law of univers e that control.

You the
«presen
ce,I
am»
Created

the law

of

univers

e And

then

you

come in

a

human

body to

experim
ent the
reality
that you
have

created.

What
you
feel,

you
attract

What
you
imagine
,
you

create

What

you

think,
you
become
.

You are

«I am»

God is

«I am»

How

can i be
"I am"?
TO BE "I
am"
YOU

MUST
LET GO
your
beliefs
All that

is
untrue!
ALL
THAT IS
NOT

YOU, IS NOT THE I AM

because

you are

the I am

when

you are

in the I
am you
feel
blissful
joyful

total
present
You feel
like you
have

superpo
wer!
You are
in this
body to

become

the best

and

complet

e that

you can

you are

the

presenc

e of

GOD So
why do
you
want
worry

about a
thing
that
don't
matter?

Humanit
y suffer
because
they are
not the

«true identity» Do you think

people
will
steal,
when
they

will
realize
that
they are
GOD?

You can have or create everythi ng that

you

want

but first

you

must be

the «I am» when your thought

enter in
silence
You can
become
the

Univers
e. This
is why
meditati
on is

powerful, but meditation is a natural

state of being. Simply being in unity

with the

moment

!

When

you let

go the
false
belief
that
God are

in the

sky.

YOU

WILL

FEEL IT

IN
YOURS
ELF
When
you feel

it in
yourself
you
know
this is

yourself when you know this is

yourself

You

accomp

lish the

miracle

that you
want!
But to
be Unite
to God

you got
to be
Unite to
yourself
to

become the «I am» you just need to

stop the

mechan

ical

works

of the

over
thinking
when
the
mind

and the

sense

are in

harmon

y you

can be

the I am

be

totally

present

Be
totally
in the
present
with

humility

with joy

and

love. To

change

or Save
humanit
y this is
not an
outside

savior it

is an

inside

savior

Yourself

. Just
accepti
ng to be
And the
rest will

come

with

grace.

Nothing

greater

than

that can

come to

you

«the

peace

of mind,

uncondi

tional

love »

love
yourself
uncondi
tionally.
.. THEN

love
everybo
dy,your
friends,
your

family!
SHARE YOUR PRESEN
T With

the
world!
To
totally
be the

«I am» Fears will disappe ar. AND

love will
replace
him. I
am
That, I

am

REPEAT

THIS

WORD

AND

IMAGIN
E WHO
YOU
ARE I
AM

THAT, I
AM
TAKE A
DEEP
BREATH

I AM
THAT, I
AM
CLOSE
YOUR

EYES

AND

VISUALI

SE I AM

THAT I

AM
Take a
deep
breath
and

found
the
peace
of your
true

identity

Let go

everythi

ng to

stop

you

from

being

the true

essence

. We
just
want BE
BE THE
PRESEN

CE OF

GOD BE

LIGHT

AND

JOY BE

THE «I AM»

God is

LOVE

GOD IS

LOVE

IF

YOU

BECOM

E

THE
I AM
YOU

become
LOVE

AND

EVERY THING YOU WANT

WILL
MANIFE
ST
ITSELF.